DOGS
IN GALLERIES

© 2003
Ministero per i Beni e le Attività Culturali
Soprintendenza Speciale per il Polo Museale Fiorentino

a publication by
s i l l a b e s.r.l.
Livorno
www.sillabe.it
info@sillabe.it

texts: Maddalena De Luca and Maddalena Paola Winspeare
managing editor: Maddalena Paola Winspeare
graphic design and drawings: Susanna Coseschi
editing: Giulia Bastianelli
translation: Bob Learmonth

reproduction rights: Archivio fotografico SSPMF; Archivio
Sillabe: Foto Paolo Nannoni, Foto Fiorenzo Luchini, Foto Tosi;
Foto Antonio Quattrone

the Publisher is at the disposal of the copyright holders of
images from unidentified sources

acknowledgements:
Kirsten Aschengreen Piacenti, Monica Bietti, Simonella Condemi,
Simona Di Marco, Adriana Fabbricatore, Giovanna Giusti, Helena
Salerno, Emilio Savelli, Maria Sframeli, Marilena Tamassia

ISBN 88-8347-199-7

Quotations on pages 16, 23, 29, 42, 50, 55 are freely translated from
T. Mann, Cane e padrone, Oscar Mondadori - Scrittori del
Novecento, Milano 2002

DOGS
IN GALLERIES

FIRENZE
MVSEI

sillabe

I met Mina one bright October morning on the seafront at Marina di Pisa. She did not look like a dog: she was walking on all fours, frenetically smelling the ground in the hope of finding familiar smells there. I stopped to watch her for a little, at first curious and then more and more worried because I detected, in that obsessive sniffing, signs of being lost and abandoned. In fact, the shopkeepers of the place told me the dog had been seen all morning going around that part of the coast with her nose down and a frightened expression as if she didn't recognise either the place or the people.

That morning Mina became my dog. Or rather: my initial intention was to find her a home that possibly was not my own; I had always wanted a dog, but work commitments had up to then made me desist from having one. However, that same day I became ill and Mina kept me company for all of the following week that I spent home.

Now I am no longer able to remember what life was like before Mina, who now spends the days in the office with me, shares my joy and anger, looks me straight in the eye to find out what mood I am in, because her future depends on my mood.

To her and all the animals that have gladdened and go on gladdening our lives, I dedicate this volume.

One often hears – especially from people who do not have them – that we cannot love them the way we love human beings. Of course it's true; the value of human life has no equal. But I can say that the experience of affection that has matured with Mina in these three years of living together has made my life better and, probably, has also made me a better person.

M. P. W.

Man's companion from far off times and equally far back is to be found the presence of the dog in figurative art. Among well–known examples, referring to the medieval period, are the famous sheepdogs – in fact more like *greyhounds* – of Giotto (Padua, Scrovegni Chapel, *Jacob's Dream* - fig.1) but also the naturalistic representation of the dog turning its vigilant look towards its master and the flock in the mosaic of the *Nativity of Christ* in Santa Maria in Trastevere, a work by Pietro Cavallini (fig. 2).

Still linked to its primary function, for which from wolf it was transformed into protector of the flock and tran–sformed man from a simple hunter into a shepherd, we find it in Andrea Pisano's panel, *Jabal, the Shepherd King* (fig. 3), for Giotto's bell–tower.

Between the 14th and 15th century, at the time of the international Gothic, the need to represent daily life with ever greater realism, yet limited to the exclusive world of the courts, imposed a study and an early classification of the breeds, like that made by Pisanello in the study of dogs preserved in the Louvre; *mastiffs, Pomerians* and *greyhounds* seem abundantly widespread and appear already distinctively in their different roles: for hunting, company and self–defence.

Bourgeois interiors, reconstructed with a wealth of detail by Flemish artists in the 15th century, emphasise dogs hav–ing become symbols of domestic intimacy: the most famous of all, the *griffon terrier* in the *Arnolfini Marriage* by Jan Van Eyck (London, National Gallery) (fig. 5), takes up a cheeky foreground position, also imprinting a slight movement on the rigorously controlled static quality of the scene.

Also holy subjects in Flemish art take on a less stately character; therefore references to real environments and landscapes also concern domestic animals. This is the case with *Madonna and Child, Saints and Donors* by Gerard David (London, National Gallery) (fig. 6) with the little *greyhound* lying down in front of his master, that ends up assuming a foreground position at the feet of the enthroned Madonna.

While in Italy Piero della Francesca, Mantegna and Vittore Carpaccio (*Vision of St Augustine*, Venice, detail of the series of San Giorgio degli Schiavoni – fig. 4) celebrate in ducal frescoes, panels and canvases the glories of dogs by now perfectly acclimatised, even in symbolic contexts (in the Malatesta Temple in Rimini, Malatesta is facing St Sigismund with his two *greyhounds*, one white the other black), and Albrecht Dürer more or less at the same time draws a *Madonna of the animals* (Vienna, Albertina) (fig. 7) with moving naturalness: a *Pomeranian* and a French *poodle* so dressed up (shaved on the back half of the body) appear at the feet of this country Madonna.

In the Renaissance period the acquisition by dogs of a definite *status* is confirmed by official portraits, where noblemen and women do not give up their precious hunting dog, huge *mastiff*, agile *greyhound* or little com–panion dog. The latter, of necessity associated with ladies and young boys, always appears with ribbons or collars *en pendant* on the clothes of the mistress or young masters: a sign, also, of a progressive transforma–tion of the animal into a precious 'object', even becom–ing a collector's item.

Meanwhile, there is no sacred or profane representation that is a little complex that does not include one or more portraits of dogs. In *Supper at Emmaus* by Veronese (Paris, Musée du Louvre) (fig. 8), dogs are not restricted to a simple begging presence at the foot of the table, but are subject of the loving care of young boys who fondle them or even take care of their coats with cloths. Moreover the artist must have particularly loved this domestic ani–mal, when even a dramatic subject like *Susanna and the Elders* (Vienna, Kunsthistorisches Museum) (fig. 9) sees the central presence of a small sized dog to which is even entrusted the safeguard of its chaste mistress.

This animal of modest size, a bit like a *spaniel* turns up in numerous canvases with a mythological subject by

Tintoretto and Titian, so that it is also called *Vecellio*. In *Venus of Urbino* in the Uffizi, crouched at the feet of its stretched out mistress, it symbolises married fidelity. Alongside this function, which it carries out perfectly (the dog is *par excellence* faithful), it is represented in the tapestries in noble private rooms, in the role that is most congenial to it of companion in daily life (Alessandro Allori, Pitti Palace, Apartment of Tapestries, 'Loggetta').

The centuries of the great courts and absolute power (17th and 18th) see the roles consolidated of the companion and hunting dogs, *mastiff* or *greyhound*. From the most famous royal portraits (Diego Velázquez, *Las Meninas*, Madrid, Prado - fig. 10), to those of nobles who had themselves immortalised by famous artists, all show the animal, by now a status symbol. The case of small-sized dogs, cult figures for kings and queens and offered as gifts like authentic jewels is emblematic of a fashion that tends to confirm dogs and masters. In the famous *Portrait of the Duchess of Alba* (fig. 11) by Francisco Goya, the noble lady and the *Bolognese bichon* both have a red bow, which the little dog wears charmingly knotted to its left back paw.

Similarly, in a bourgeois environment, dogs are the necessary complement of domestic settings and scenes of daily life (Pietro Longhi, *The tailor*, Venice, Galleria dell'Accademia - fig. 12) when indeed they themselves are not the main subject in the work: in *The morning of a young woman* (Frans Jansz van Mieris I, St Petersburg, The Hermitage) (fig. 13) the affectionate demonstration by the dog, that carries out the order given by the woman with a snap of her fingers standing up on two paws, is the real subject of the picture rather than the mistress' toilet or what the servant is doing.

The neo-classic 19th century brings back splendid sculptural groups that accentuate the quick flexibility of a dog's anatomy (Antonio Canova, *Sleep of Endymion*, Chatsworth, Devonshire Collection - fig. 14), while from the middle of the century, following the impetus of English society that conferred a fundamental role on the dog in its own daily life, the selection of breeds was increased and, consequently, their classification. So in pictures various types of hunting animals appear just like different breeds of companion dogs, reproduced with ever greater attention to naturalistic detail.

Contemporary art presents more complex patterns of change and the different artistic currents that succeed each other in the 20th century impose just as many semantic values as their subjects. The dog conforms now becoming a purely formal value (Douanier Rousseau, *Country wedding* - fig. 15), now taking on again its primary symbolic value (Carlo Carrà, *The wait* - fig. 16).

In art, like in literature, the vocabulary that describes man's companion gives voice to the world of intimate, discreet affection. The sense of time passing, the importance of memory in the identity of the individual, become more and more tangible towards the unchangeable loyalty of the dog and the fussy repetition of its daily habits:

Il sole lentamente si sposta
sulla nostra vita, sulla paziente
storia dei giorni che un mite
calore accende, d'affetti e di memorie.

A quest'ora meridiana
lo spaniel invecchia sul mattone
tiepido, il tuo cappello di paglia
s'allontana nell'ombra della casa.

(The sun shifts slowly on our life, on the patient history that a mild warmth lights up, with affection and memories. At this afternoon hour the spaniel is growing old on the warm bricks and with your old straw hat goes away into the shade of the house.)

(Attilio Bertolucci, *At home* from Lettera da casa)

M. P. W.

one

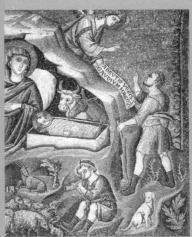

two

four

three

five

six

seven

eight

nine

ten

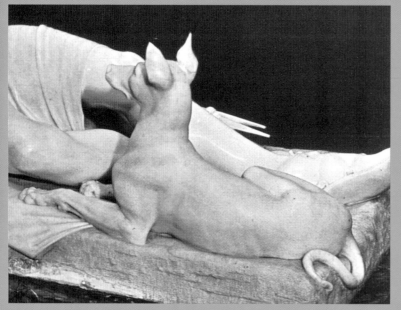

fifteen

sixteen

"A strange soul! So friendly and yet so apart, so different in many ways that our words show they are unable to do justice to this logic".

16

Andrea di Bonaiuto, *Triumph of the Church*. Florence, Santa Maria Novella, Spanish Chapel

Giovanni da Milano, *Meeting of Saint Joachim and Saint Anne*, detail of the *Stories of the Virgin*. Florence, Santa Croce, Rinuccini Chapel

Lorenzo Monaco, *Adoration of the Magi*. Florence, Uffizi Gallery

Pontormo, *Vertumnus and Pomona*. Poggio a Caiano, Medici Villa

Pastoral scene, from the series of *Spring*, tapestry after a drawing and a cartoon by Alessandro Allori (?). Florence, Pitti Palace

Giovan Battista Benigni, *Portrait of the Martelli family*. Florence, Martelli Palace

"It is the law [...] of his life to run only when I am moving too and to stand still as soon as I stop".

Benozzo Gozzoli, *Procession of the Magi*. Florence, Medici Riccardi Palace

Paolo Uccello, *Battle of San Romano*. Florence, Uffizi Gallery

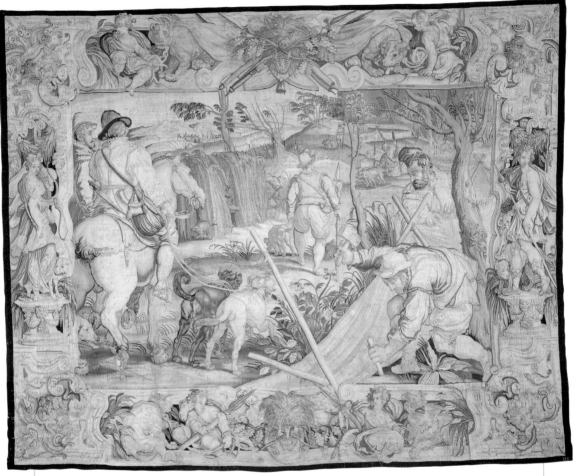

Grey-goose hunting, tapestry after a drawing and a cartoon by Allori. Florence, Pitti Palace

Wild boar hunting with "nets", tapestry after a drawing and a cartoon by Giovanni Stradano. Florence, Pitti Palace

Following page:
Porcupine hunting with "the hoe", tapestry after a drawing and a cartoon by Giovanni Stradano. Florence, Pitti Palace

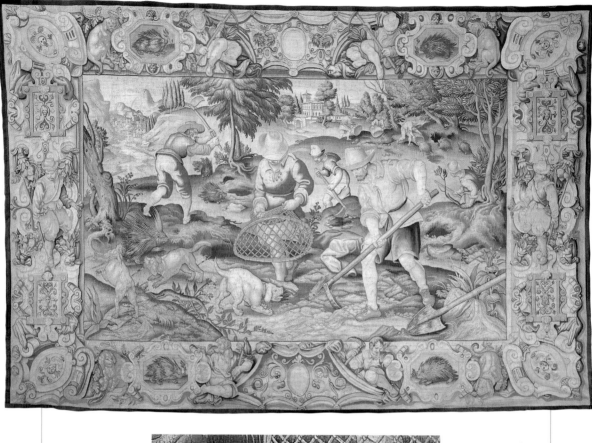

"He stretches himself almost to breaking point and, to spin it out, divides the undertaking into two parts. Firstly he spreads out his front legs, in the meantime sending his hind quarters up in the air, then takes care of them by extending and opening wide his other two legs. The two phases are accompanied by very vulgar yawns with jaws wide open".

29

Titian, *Venus and Cupid.* Florence, Uffizi Gallery

Tintoretto, *Leda and the Swan.* Florence, Uffizi Gallery

16th-century anonymous Flemish painter, *Two women in the kitchen*. Florence, Palatine Gallery (depository)

Frederick Sustris, *Birth scene*. Florence, Palatine Gallery

Alessandro Allori, *Banquet of Cleopatra*. Florence, Palazzo Vecchio, Study of Francesco I

Alessandro Fei, *The goldsmith's shop*. Florence, Palazzo Vecchio, Study of Francesco I

Jacopo Chimenti da Empoli, *Saint Eligius and King Clovis*. Florence, Uffizi Gallery

Leandro Bassano (school of), *Market scene*. Florence, Medici Villa of Petraia

Leandro Bassano (school of), *Allegory of the elements: Earth*. Florence, Uffizi Gallery (depository)

Wild boar hunting with musket,
tapestry after a drawing and a
cartoon by Giovanni Stradano.
Florence, Pitti Palace

Pietro da Cortona, *The Age of Gold*. Florence, Pitti Palace, Stove Room

Adriano Cecioni, *The master's exit*. Florence, Modern Art Gallery

"As always when I am with him, my heart is full of joy and liking".

42

Preceeding page:
Alessandro Allori, fresco of the Loggetta vault. Florence, Pitti Palace

These pages:
Pieter Brueghel, *Farmhouse feast*. Florence, Stibbert Museum

Dosso Dossi, *Allegory of Hercules*. Florence, Uffizi Gallery

Livio Mehus, *Satirical scene*. Florence, Pitti Palace

Niccolò Cassana, *The cook*. Florence, Uffizi Gallery, Vasari's Corridor

Giambattista Tiepolo, *Erecting a statue in honour of an emperor.* Florence, Uffizi Gallery

Vittorio Corcos, *The daughter of Jack la Bolina*. Florence, Modern Art Gallery

"He's there watching me and listening to my tone of voice, in raptures with the emphasis of the definite agreement about his existence that I'm lavishing on him with what I'm saying".

Federico Barocci, *Madonna of the People*. Florence, Uffizi Gallery

Bernardino Poccetti, *Wedding at Cana*. Badia a Ripoli, Convento dell'Immacolata Concezione della Provvidenza

German manufacture, *Knife-grinder*. Florence, Silverworks Museum

Elizabeth Chaplin, *Nenette on a bench*. Florence, Modern Art Gallery

"All his life is waiting, waiting for the next walk in the open air and his anxiety starts again as soon as he has rested after the previous one".

55

Gentile da Fabriano, *Adoration of the Magi*. Florence, Uffizi Gallery

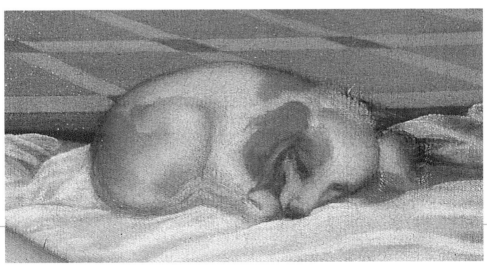

Preceeding page:
Tiziano, *Venus of Urbino*. Florence, Uffizi Gallery

These pages:
Gerrit Dou, *Woman selling fritters*, Florence, Uffizi Gallery
17th-century unknown, *Dog asleep*. Florence, Pitti Palace

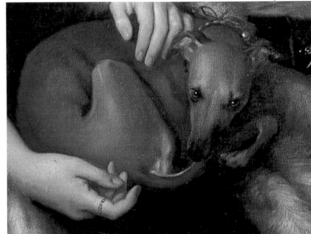

Giuseppe Bezzuoli, *Portrait of a lady*. Florence, Gallery of Palazzo Mozzi-Bardini

Paolo Freccia, *Love and fidelity*. Florence, Modern Art Gallery

Augusto Betti, *Supper at Emmaus*. Florence, Museum of the Medici Chapels

Together with the valuable collections that show the presence of dogs in the ways described above, full supplementary information on the Medici court could not ignore the presence of animals in general and the domestic animal par excellence, the dog. With regard to this are emblematic the tapestries and, in particular, the series of hunts made by "Creati Fiorentini" to designs and cartoons by Giovanni Stradano. The Flemish painter and engraver, having moved to Florence in about 1545, imprinted on the fabric images the vividness and pathos that different types of hunt require, also indulging in especially successful realistic details.

Far from forming a subsidiary index, dogs return in full force to the record, therefore also to the documents preserved and the abundant patrimony handed down, through which court life at the time of the Medici can be reconstructed. And this is why a section of this brief excursus concerns the many pictures kept in deposits. They are portraits to be "glanced through" like a family album, affectionate domestic presences to which about twenty years ago a beautiful exhibition called *Natura viva* was dedicated to emphasise that characteristic of throbbing vitality extraneous to much more numerous (and famous) still-lifes.

M. P. W.

63

1) Tiberio Titi, *Dogs of the Medici family in Boboli Gardens*. London, private collection

Court dogs
Collars and dogs of the Medici family

Like a family album, from paintings in the collections of the House of the Medici, the images of so many dogs and puppies jump out at you, often beside the little prince or princess, rigidly fixed in a pose before the court portraitist or faithfully crouched at the feet of the young and elderly ladies of the family. In some cases we are surprised to see them portrayed in pride of place, accurately and we might almost say with insight into their character, by the same painters that had immortalised their masters.

The way of having near one a little dog was in keeping with what was happening in the great European courts, where Mary Queen of Scots, the Duchess of Orleans, Henrietta of England owned little salon dogs.

Also in this the Medici grand dukes were on a level with the princes of Europe, as the numerous family portraits show with little dogs such as *spaniels*, *pugs*, *Bolognese breeds*, *Dalmatians*.

Right from the 16th century the grand dukes imported semi-precious stones for mosaic works, received tulip bulbs from Holland and Jasmine, called the 'Grand Duke of Tuscany' (i.e. Arabian Jasmine), that had been sent from Goa to Cosimo III to enrich the gardens of the Villa of Castello; probably already from the beginnings of the dynasty English bred dogs had arrived from England.

The care of these small-sized companion dogs was entrusted to dwarves who combed them, decorated them with little bows and, as can be seen in the amusing canvas set in the amphitheatre of Boboli Gardens, often dressed them up with earrings and brooches. In this painting (*Dogs of the Medici family in Boboli Gardens* - fig. 1), made known by Marco Chiarini on the occasion of the exhibition *Curiosità di una reggia*

(1979, card no. 31), the dwarf has on his knees a box a little *spaniel* is coming out of, also adorned with bows. All over the place the same dogs are to be seen in portraits, like the white *spaniel* in the centre and the one lying down beside the dwarf, or little dogs with long ears and big eyes that look towards us and have a beautiful collar with studs or a real jewel attached to the hair on their ear (in the bottom left of the painting). In the centre, still and quiet, but secured by a lead with a studded collar, stands a bigger dog (perhaps a *Molossian hound*) that seems to put up with the liveliness of the little dogs surrounding it.

In portraits of ladies and young princes very often *pugs* appear, or little *spaniels* or a *Bolognese*. But breeds evolved through the centuries so that some other types of dogs, that we find in the 16th- and 17th-century paintings, for example the *spaniel*, are different today: in the case of the *lion-dog*, the breed is extinct (*Dhers and Rufer, Chien de garde, de Berger, de luxe, Lévriers et Terriers*, Paris 1956).

Maria Maddalena of Austria, portrayed in widow's clothes, in an austere pose, has at her feet a little white *spaniel*, the only sign of affection in so much decorum (fig. 2). The little dog, with long white hair seems to be the same that is in the arms of her daughter Anna de' Medici (K. Langedijk, I, no. 3, p. 248) (fig. 12) and it is undoubtedly the one portrayed in ivory, with long ears and long white hair (fig. 16).

A *Bolognese dog* is portrayed with great vividness and dare we say 'psychological insight' by the official court portrait-painter Justus Suttermans on a red velvet dais, almost a stage, with also a red, half-open curtain. Here it can be clearly seen how long the hair

is on the head and neck, whereas on the body and paws the hair is cropped (fig. 15).

Also two *spaniels*, dressed up for the occasion, with a beautiful bow on the ear (inv. 1890 no. 4737) (fig. 3), have been given the honour of a 'personal' portrait by Suttermans, who often inserted them beside the important people portrayed. Probably the little pictures only with dogs were for the court painter a preliminary study that was used later.

To the breed of *spaniel*, in all probability, belonged the little dog published by Marilena Mosco (*Natura Viva,* card no. 25) with its stud collar, similar to what is described in the Medici inventories (fig. 4). The characteristic of wavy hair on the head, ears and neck and sleek on the rest of the body, makes me think that it is really a question of this breed, so many times portrayed in court paintings. The little dog has a mottled white and tawny coat with big eyes out of proportion to its little body: in Suttermans' portrait in Brussels, Maria Maddalena of Austria holds a little animal with one hand which is as big as the dog (K. Langedijk, II, no. 90, p. 1285).

With this type of dog beside them had been portrayed three children of Ferdinando I: Claudia (Suttermans, fig. 11) Eleonora (Tiberio, Titi [?], Vienna, Kunsthistorisches Museum, see K. Langedijk, I, no. 32, p. 680) and Carlo (unknown artist, private collection; K. Langedijk, I, no 15, p. 335). Claudia, already grown-up and standing with the bearing of a princess, has a little dog at her feet, who erect with its little collar with a stud in the middle, looks at the observer; the child Eleonora leans her hand on a little table covered with cloth on which is placed a vase of flowers and there is a little dog, still and quiet like a knick-knack; Carlo, portrayed at the age of ten with a red 'Turkish suit' and so occupied in front of the painter

that he is not concerned about the dog so that it seems to have been put into the painting by chance.

Suttermans had also portrayed Maria Maddalena of Austria's son Leopoldo (inv. 1890 no. 3660) with a sceptre in his hand and a parrot free on the table on his right and at his feet a little dog that looks like a sort of *spaniel*.

Also young Vittoria della Rovere, the fiancée of Ferdinando II de' Medici, would be portrayed in Urbino with a similar little dog, but a bit bigger (fig. 6).

The *pug*, also a little salon dog, is the faithful companion in the silent life of Ferdinando I's widow, Christine of Lorraine, as appears in the painting where the grand duchess is intent on prayer (fig. 5). The white animal, lying on the floor strewn with flowers, in contrast with the long black train of its mistress, looks towards the observer, fixed in a pose.

Also the *pug*, like other dogs in the noble house, has had the honour of being portrayed alone, but this time in a special way. Indeed, perhaps because of its small size, it is inserted into a still-life by a woman painter devoted to this type of work, Giovanna Garzoni (fig. 17): in the parchment it is almost as small as the cup and biscuit set on the table where the dog is lying.

When the young princes are a little bigger, having given up their games with little dogs, they are already devoted to the art of hunting and are portrayed with hounds, as is Francesco Maria, Vittoria della Rovere's son, who, in Suttermans' portrait, has beside him a *Molossian*, with a very solid collar, given the fierceness of the breed, with a decoration of studs (inv. 1890 no. 9796) (fig. 7).

Another *Molossian* is depicted in a group of dogs, with a collar we might call 'armed' to enhance its dangerous bite (inv. 1890 no. 4865) (fig. 19).

The young prince Francesco, also son of Maria

Maddalena of Austria, is portrayed with a *Dalmatian*, also a companion dog rather than for hunting and with an affectionate gesture holds his little child's hand on the dog's head. The same type of *Dalmatian*, white with black spots, in another big canvas in the Pitti Palace depository, is kept on a lead by a dwarf that has a mace in his right hand (inv. 1890 no. 2452) (fig. 8).

On a red silk cushion with gold thread tassels at the corners is set, for the court portraitist Tiberio Titi, a *greyhound*, also with a refined collar with metal decoration (fig. 14). A *greyhound*, a dog suited to hunting, also appears in the portrait of the Electress Palatine, who in hunting dress and a rifle in her right hand is shown to us today just as she probably appeared in the numerous hunting parties in the Palatinate that she took part in together with her husband Wilhelm von Pfalz. In the same painting there is also present a tawny-coloured French *spaniel* that in another canvas attributed to Pandolfo Reschi has been portrayed lying down, sleeping: here, whatever trace of austerity there is has disappeared and the little animal is relishing its sleep indifferent to the royal presence.

The *gun-dog* or 'spotted dog' as it is described in the inventories of the Medici Guardaroba, even if not of noble breed it was a villa dog and for this reason has also perhaps gained the privilege of being portrayed alone with a beautiful collar placed on the side even with the Medici coat of arms and studs (fig. 9). The canvas was originally in Lorenzo de' Medici's Picture Gallery; he seems to have been fond of dogs (*Quadreria di Don Lorenzo de' Medici*, Florence 1977, card no. 46, p. 71). Hounds used to faithfully accompany the princes and grand dukes in hunting parties at the villas of Artimino, Petraia or Poggio a Caiano, as can be seen from the painting, preserved today at the Carabinieri Centre in Rome, with in the foreground a hunter holding on a lead a *gun-dog* with a collar with the Medici coat of arms (inv. 1890 no. 6862).

Just how important the collars of their dogs were considered by Medici princes is demonstrated by the fact that the inventory, made on the death of the Great Prince Ferdinando, which among other things lists important paintings, sculptures and precious art objects, opens with a description of two collars: "a silver-plated dog collar… a similar one in gilded silver plate linked above other in copper-plate with arms and the royal crown, a stud for the bell and words in silver (*Inventario dei Mobili e delle Masserizie della proprietà del Serenissimo Signore Principe Ferdinando di Gloriosa ricordanza… 1713*; Archivio di Stato di Firenze, Medici Guardaroba 1222, c. 1).

Collars similar to the second listed above are found in the group of hunting dogs, with a cat and a rabbit, where a hunting *griffon* appears, a very powerful animal, with long tawny-coloured hair (fig. 19). One point strengthens the hypothesis that it is a question of dogs belonging to the Medici: the *griffon* in fact appears in a portrait with a child of the noble family (fig. 13). The painting with the child dressed in red, with a curtain on the right, seems to have to be dated, like lots of other portraits of the young princes, to the early 17th century, while the figure of the servant that restrains the *griffon* on the right of the picture might have been inserted some decades later because the servant holding the animal is exactly similar to "hunchbacked little Christopher" who has in his hand a plate of spinach in the canvas painted by Gabbiani around 1684 (*Curiosità di una reggia*, card no. 27).

M. D. L.

2) Justus Suttermans, *Portrait of Maria Maddalena d'Austria*. Medici Villa of Poggio a Caiano

3) Justus Suttermans, *Two dogs with bows*. Florence, Pitti Palace (depository)

4) Justus Suttermans (attr.), *Portrait of a dog*. Medici Villa of Poggio a Caiano (depository)

5) Franco Bianchi Buonavita, *Portrait of Christine of Lorraine*. Florence, Pitti Palace (depository)

6) 17th-century painter, *Portrait of Vittoria della Rovere.* Florence, Uffizi Gallery, Vasari's Corridor

7) Justus Suttermans, *Portrait of Francesco Maria de' Medici.* Florence, Uffizi Gallery (depository)

8) 17th-century Florentine painter, *Dwarf with a dog.* Florence, Pitti Palace (depository)

9) Tiberio Titi (attr.), *Spotted dog.* Florence, Pitti Palace (depository)

10) Justus Suttermans, *Portrait of Leopoldo de' Medici*. Florence, Uffizi Gallery (depository)

11) Justus Suttermans, *Portrait of Claudia de' Medici*. Florence, Medici Villa of Petraia

12) Justus Suttermans, *Portrait of Anna de' Medici*. Florence, Uffizi Gallery (depository)

13) 17th-century Florentine painter, *Portrait of the young Prince with a servant and dog*. Florence, Pitti Palace (depository)

14) Tiberio Titi (attr.), *Female dog*, Florence, Pitti Palace (depository)
15) Justus Suttermans (attr.), *Portrait of a Bolognese dog*. Florence, Pitti Palace (depository)

16) Florentine manufacture, *Dog*. Florence, Silverworks Museum
17) Giovanna Garzoni, *Small dog with cup and biscuits*. Florence, Palatine Gallery

18) Jan van Kessel (attr.), *Still-life with a monkey stealing fruit.* Florence, Palatine Gallery

19) 17th-century painter, *Portrait of dogs, cat, and rabbit*. Florence, Pitti Palace (depository)

20) Jan Fyt (school of), *Three cats and a dog*. Florence, Pitti Palace (depository)
21) Cristoforo Munari (attr.), *Still-life of fruit and vegetables, with dog and cat*. Florence, Pitti Palace (depository)

essential bibliography

Inventario dei Mobili e delle Masserizie della proprietà del Serenissimo Signore Principe Ferdinando di Gloriosa ricordanza… 1713, Archivio di Stato di Firenze, Guardaroba Medicea 1222, c. 1

J. Dhers, F. Rufer, *Chien de garde, de Berger, de luxe, Lévriers et Terriers*, Paris 1956

La quadreria di Don Lorenzo de' Medici, exhibition catalogue (Poggio a Caiano), edited by E. Borea, Florence 1977

Curiosità di una reggia. Vicende della guardaroba di Palazzo Pitti, exhibition catalogue (Florence), Florence 1979

K. Langedijk, *The Portaits of the Medici. 15th-18th Centuries*, Florence 1981-1983, voll. 2

Natura viva in casa Medici, exhibition catalogue (Florence), edited by M. Mosco, Florence 1985

R. Orsi Landini in *I principi bambini: abbigliamento e infanzia nel Seicento*, exhibition catalogue (Florence), Florence 1985

C. d'Anthenaise, P. de Fougerolle, K. MacDonogh, M.-C. Prestat, *Vies de Chiens*, Paris 2000

L. Zaczek, *Les chiens dans l'art, la photographie et la litérature*, Köln 2000

W. Record, *A breed apart. The art collections of The American Kennel Club and The American Kennel Club Museum of The Dog*, Woodbridge 2001

Il giuramento del Senato Fiorentino a Ferdinando II de' Medici. Una grande opera del Suttermans restaurata, edited by C. Caneva e M. Vervat, Florence 2002

Mina... in Boboli!

printed
in October 2003
by Genesi
Città di Castello (PG)
for s i l l a b e